a passion for

Shoes

Emma Bowd

RYLAND
PETERS
& SMALL

LONDON NEW YORK

To Mum.

Designer Luis Peral-Aranda
Editor Miriam Hyslop
Location Research Manager Kate Brunt
Production Patricia Harrington
Art Director Gabriella Le Grazie
Publishing Director Alison Starling

First published in the United Kingdom in 2002
by Ryland Peters & Small
20–21 Jockey's Fields, London WC1R 4BW
www.rylandpeters.com

10 9 8

Text © Emma Bowd 2002
Design and photographs © Ryland Peters & Small 2002

Printed and bound in China.

ISBN 978 1 84172 352 5

A CIP record for this book is available from
the British Library.

contents

Shoes make a lot of women happy. In fact, we love them. They are our faithful friends that travel life's many winding roads with us each day. Just to be able to glance down and marvel at their sheer beauty lifts our spirits, irrespective of the many obstacles in our way.

first shoes

Our love affair with shoes often takes hold at a very, very young age. Most people cannot resist buying pretty little pairs of shoes for newborn baby girls, despite the fact that they cannot walk yet, and a pair of socks or booties would suffice – at a fraction of the cost. These shoes will usually be ill-fitting and serve no real purpose in life, other than to sit on a shelf and look absolutely gorgeous in all their flowery and butterfly-embroidered glory. Sound familiar? We are products of our environment after all! By the time of toddler-hood the seeds of the romance are often fully sown, ready to blossom into a lifetime of shoe-wearing bliss.

Like every little girl before us with a love of pretty shoes, we go on to appreciate the subtle nuances of these most marvellous of inventions. It will soon become gloriously clear that a pair of designer high heels equates with instant glamour; that sandals

a fine romance

symbolize happy carefree summers; that brightly coloured shoes cheer up even the dreariest days; and that slippers have magical powers capable of making the worries of the world simply melt away. Shoes are truly the foundations of a lifetime's happy, fond memories.

best foot forward

The avid female shoe connoisseur is absolutely convinced of her prowess when it comes to assessing the personality of a stranger at fifty paces - or however close she needs to be to see their shoes! We've come a long way from the days of tying a bit of leather and vine around our feet in the dim light of the cave. The styles of shoes we choose to wear speak a thousand words about how we wish the world to perceive us. Kitten heels, spiky stilettos, toe-crunching mules, platform wedges, chunky clogs, two-toned brogues, satin logo-encrusted slippers, leopard-print loafers, strappy sequined sandals, fake leather, patent leather, natural leather, purple leather

- all give away vital clues about the person within. And nowhere do we use the skill of putting our best foot forward more effectively than in the all-important job interview. Here, you will invariably present yourself in your best pair of shoes. Not too high,

well-heeled

not too low, perfectly matching your outfit, polished, fashionable and under-stated, reliable and sophisticated. Everything you want your prospective new boss to know about you without actually having to say a single word! Your choice of shoe can speak volumes.

the thrill of the chase

*C*an there be a more enjoyable way for the shoe-lover to spend a Saturday morning than experiencing the adrenalin rush of a shoe sale? Better still, not simply any old shoe sale, but the phenomenal 'designer' shoe sale. In this situation one of two moods will envelop you. First, there is the 'sensible' mood whereby you purchase the comfortable and classic pump, which you will wear forever, and could not otherwise have afforded to buy if it was not at a reduced price. Alternately, there is the ridiculous 'I-can't-possibly-leave-this-store-until-I-have-bought-something' mood. It is in this frame of mind that you will find yourself paying out most of your

month's grocery money for a new pair of shoes. A gorgeous pair of green, satin Jimmy Choo mules, for example, with a frighteningly high heel (that you have no chance of ever being able to walk in without applying super-glue to the soles of your feet) that are

moments of madness

a size too small and don't match a single outfit in your wardrobe. It doesn't matter - they were half price, and they are Jimmy Choos for goodness sake. The thrill of the chase can provoke moments of madness in even the most rational of women!

skyscraper stiletto

Other than the female human, no mammal on earth would consider maiming and torturing themselves in an effort to gain an extra three inches of height. But as any woman knows, the rewards of high heels far outweigh the costs. Height is desirable. Height is power. Throughout history, what red-blooded male has ever been able to resist the alluring, magnetic pull of the female form gently swaying and swirling its way past him on skyscraper stilettos in a little black dress? From the moment you slip on your sassy, razor sharp Manolos the world is truly your oyster. Well almost – as long as you avoid parquet floors and grass verges!

the favourite shoe

In the eyes of the shoe-lover the 'all-time-favourite shoe' is the pair of shoes you just can't throw out, because you hope in your heart of hearts that two-tone sailor shoes will come back into fashion one day. Or, they are the shoes that you wished you had bought two pairs of because you've already had them resoled three times and it is just not possible to milk one more season out of them. Conversely, a seasonal favourite can be a pair of shoes that you buy at the beginning of the summer and wear every single time you leave the house. Irrespective of whether or not they match your outfit. You just love them. Even though you've got 20 other pairs

the temple

The genuine shoe-lover has a bulging collection of shoes that vary in colour, shape, material, price and height. And there is no greater measure of your devotion to your shoes than the way you care for and store them. Do you lovingly wax and polish and resole your shoes before they start to wear little holes that you can suddenly feel the pavement through? Or would the state of your shoes be more accurately described as tatty and well loved at best? Or are your shoes thrown into the bottom of your wardrobe to form a mangled heap like Mount Vesuvius following an eruption? Did you re-mortgage your house and sell your

car so that you could afford one of those trendy, super-organized built-in wardrobes, where every pair of shoes has its own special little dedicated shelf or drawer? The truly devoted amongst us; however, will always ask to keep the shoeboxes and paste small

shoe princess

photographs on the outside of the box just to remind us of its contents once neatly packed away in our wardrobes. If hiding your beautiful bounty behind closed doors is not your style, then don't hesitate to enjoy their company with open display storage.

the party shoe

If ever an excuse is needed to buy a new pair of shoes, then surely a party is the ultimate! It is the perfect opportunity to sideline those sensible work shoes and be carried away by the frivolity of the occasion. Designers delight in luring us with dizzying arrays of divine party shoes in delicate fabrics, trimmed with diamanté butter-flies, exquisite glass beads, faux pearls, and sparkling sequins. The goal of any party shoe is of course glamour. At all costs. It doesn't matter if you cannot walk more than five steps at a time in your rhinestone-bejewelled stilts without a little rest to regain your balance and composure. Find a spot, stand there and look good.

the perfect match

The following four small words are guaranteed to bring joy to the heart of any die-hard shoe-lover...'matching shoes and handbag'. There is something truly pleasing and unquantifiable about the look and feel of the identically coloured, stitched or beaded material in all its glory, both on your feet and over your shoulder. The contribution that the matching shoes and handbag make to the transformation of a woman's whole ensemble is far greater than the sum of the parts on their own. The perfect marriage of shoes and handbag could catapult you to 'accessories nirvana', making you stand out from the crowd as the ultimate statement in style.

the holiday shoe

Why is it that we manage to pack the same number of shoes (a lot) for a weekend break to Berlin as we do for a week in Barcelona? It's quite simple really – it's a girl thing. We cannot survive happily with just one or two pairs of shoes like our male counterparts. Different shoes go with different outfits. It is best to be prepared for all foreseeable weather changes and social activities throughout the period of absence. End of story. The summer holiday is not a summer holiday without a pretty pair of sandals and painted toenails to match. A sign of a truly great holiday is the purchase of a unique pair of shoes that will

forever remind you of happy times spent abroad. All you have to do is slip into your striped, silk slippers and you are quickly transported back to a special place. The sights, the sounds and the smells of that intoxicating Turkish bazaar, for example, where you once spent hours haggling over the price of a rug, whilst sipping what seemed like endless cups of fragrant tea.

the wedding shoe

What better way to start your married life than as you mean to continue? Commissioning a pair of bespoke shoes covered in the material of your wedding gown, which will make you glide down the aisle feeling every bit the princess that you are. For the total effect you will of course have a divine little handbag made and covered in the same fabric too. The sheer luxury and indulgence is more than compensated for by the instant creation of your very first set of family heirlooms! To complete the theme, why not give your bridesmaids satin-covered evening shoes and handbags to match their dresses, as a very personal thank you gift that you

know they will be able to wear and enjoy after the big day? Wedding shoes, by their very nature, are extra-ordinary shoes that need scrupulous planning - at least as much time as that given to your gown. Sexy sling-backs may look appealing in their

dress to impress

brilliant white and feathered haze, but churches and reception venues almost always have mountains of awkward steps and slippery slopes to negotiate. Choose your shoes wisely and pencil in plenty of walking practice for a picture-perfect day!

suppliers & stockists

Charles Jourdan
27 New Bond Street
London W1S 3SW
t. 020 7629 5969
www.charles-jourdan.com

Christian Louboutin
t. 020 7823 2234 for stores

Emma Hope
53 Sloane Square
London SW1X 8AX
t. 020 7259 9566
www.emmahope.co.uk

Fenwick
New Bond Street
London W1A 3BS
t. 020 7629 9161
www.fenwick.co.uk

Gina
189 Sloane Street
London SW1X 9QR
t. 020 7235 2932
www.ginashoes.com

Gucci
t. 020 7471 4199 for stores
www.gucci.com

Harrods Ltd.
Knightsbridge
London SW1X 7XL
t. 020 7730 1234
www.harrods.com

Jesus Lopez
69 Marylebone High Street
London W1U 5JJ
t. 020 7486 7870

Jimmy Choo
169 Draycott Avenue
London SW3 3AJ
t. 020 7235 0242
www.jimmychoo.com

Joseph Azagury
73 Knightsbridge
London SW1X 7RB
t. 020 7259 9566

Liberty Plc.
Regent Street
London W1R 6AH
t. 020 7734 1234
www.liberty.co.uk

LK Bennett
t. 020 7491 3005 for stores
www.lkbennett.com

Manolo Blahnik
49–51 Old Church Street
London SW3 5BS
t. 020 7352 8622

Oasis
69–77 Paul Street
London EC2A 4PN
t. 020 7452 1000

Parallel
22 Marylebone High Street
London W1M 3PE
t. 020 7224 0441

Postmistress
61–63 Monmouth Street
London WC2H 9DG
t. 020 7370 4040

Prada
t. 020 7235 0008 / 7647 5000
    for stores

Russell & Bromley
t. 020 8460 1122 for stores
www.russellandbromley.co.uk

Selfridges & Co.
400 Oxford Street
London W1A 1AB
t. 020 7629 1234
&
1 The Dome
The Trafford Centre
Manchester MI7 8DA
t. 0161 629 1234
www.selfridges.co.uk

Shoon Ltd.
Dinder House
Dinder
Near Wells
Somerset BA5 3PB
t. 01749 686 879

Top Shop
t. 0870 122 8808 for stores
www.topshop.co.uk

Vivienne Westwood
6 Davies Street
London W1Y 1LJ
t. 020 7629 3757
www.viviennewestwood.com

credits & acknowledgements

key: *a*=above, *b*=below, *l*=left, *r*=right, *c*=centre

Special photography, front and back jacket: Chris Everard
Other photography by:
Chris Drake: *8; 54*
Chris Everard: *4-5; 11; 14; 17 br; 20; 26; 42; 46; 49*
Catherine Gratwicke: *17 bc; 18* Lulu Guiness's house in London; *23* Laura Stoddart's
apartment in London; *29; 33* VV Rouleaux, Ribbons, Trimmings and Braids; *39* Designer
Ann-Louise Roswald's apartment in London; *53*
Debi Treloar: *11; 12*
Verity Welstead: *34* Lulu Guiness's house in London
Andrew Wood: *7; 17 al; 17 ac; 17 bl; 17 ar; 36 ; endpapers*
Polly Wreford: *2; 17 lc; 17 cc; 17 cr; 24; 30; 40; 45; 50; 56; 59; 60*

Thank you to the entire team at RPS for making a small but lovely dream come true.
Special thanks to Annabel for taking me seriously in the first place; Alison and Miriam for
their support and guidance; and Gabriella, Luis and Kate for the gorgeous images.
And a million hugs to Darcey without whom this book would never have happened.
   The author and publisher would also like to thank everyone who made the photography
for this book possible. Grateful thanks to Emma Hope; Emma Hope for Paul Smith;
Jesus Lopez and Parallel for allowing us to photograph their beautiful shoes.
Special thanks to Debbie, Patricia, Susan and Julia.